Jack Rose

Jack Rose's
LOWESTOFT
PICTURE
SHOW

Rushmere
Publishing

First published 1998 by Rushmere Publishing
32 Rushmere Road, Carlton Colville, Lowestoft, Suffolk

Printed and typeset in England by Blackwell John Buckle
Charles Street, Great Yarmouth, Norfolk NR30 3LA

ISBN 1 872992 12 9

Acknowledgements

Most of the photographs in this book come from my own collection, but a few have been gratefully borrowed and for this I would like to thank Molly O'Shane, Roger Breeds, Ken Carsey and Robin Summers. I would also like to thank Dean Parkin for editing, Christine Johnson for proof-reading and Anna Hogan for the painting of Joseph Conrad.

A special word of thanks must go to Bert Collyer, who has given me the benefit of his photographic skills for many years now and I certainly appreciate his continuing help.

Dedicated to
the memory of
Ernie & Olive Graystone

(Right)
One of the late Ernie Graystone's photographs, taken in the 1970s, looking across the trawl dock towards the South Pier. The pavilion was opened in 1956 by the Duke of Edinburgh and demolished in January 1989.

The Yacht Club

The club house of the Royal Norfolk and Suffolk Yacht Club, which overlooks the yacht basin. This association established a club house in Lowestoft in 1885, due to an increase in the popularity of sea racing, and a pavilion containing a reading room and a billiards room was built on the site of the present club. By the time the club received a warrant entitling it to the 'Royal' prefix in 1898 increasing membership had rendered the old pavilion inadequate. Construction began on a new clubhouse in 1902 and when the building work cost more than expected, the extra £4,000 was provided by the Great Eastern Railway Company, the then owners of the harbour, who granted a long lease. The club would eventually buy the premises outright in 1959 from the British Transport Commission.

The old pavilion was moved to the Crown Meadow football pitch and the new clubhouse was opened by Lord Claude Hamilton on July 11th, 1903. After the opening ceremony it is reported, ". . . An adjournment was then made to the Royal Hotel for luncheon after which several accepted the invitation of the Mayor (Mr Lancelot Orde) to make a trip on the new electric tramline which had not then been opened to the public. Three cars, the first driven by the Mayor, then made the run. Others more interested in sailing took part in a handicap race round the Newcome Sands . . ."

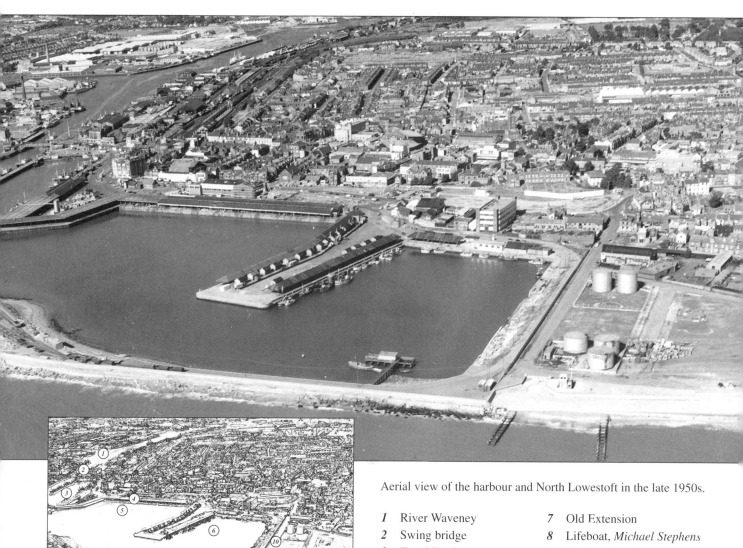

Aerial view of the harbour and North Lowestoft in the late 1950s.

1	River Waveney	*7*	Old Extension
2	Swing bridge	*8*	Lifeboat, *Michael Stephens*
3	Trawl Dock	*9*	Harbour Beach
4	Fish Market	*10*	Hamilton Road
5	Waveney Dock	*11*	Oil depot
6	Hamilton Dock	*12*	Coastguard Station

On the Fish Market in the late 1970s. The refurbishment of the market had been considered for the best part of three decades before action was taken in the mid-1980s and a new Fish Market was finally unveiled in September 1987. When this photograph was taken however the old place was looking dilapidated and certainly in need of revitalisation.

A busy scene showing drifters unloading their catches in the 1950s. After the herring had been unloaded the empty aluminium boxes would be washed out, as shown in the foreground, and then be loaded back on board in the fish room, ready for the drifters to set sail to the fishing grounds again.

The *Roy Stevens*, moored in a snowy Waveney Dock. On the last day of December, 1963, this vessel was named top Lowestoft trawler of the year, setting a new record for gross earnings at the port with her total of £44,991. This was the first trawler owned by Small & Company to win the competition, narrowly beating *Boston Buccaneer* with a margin of only £396. Named after one of the company's directors, the vessel was skippered by Tony Reynolds (inset) who had only been a skipper for two and a half years and put his success down to 'a lot of luck and a little know-how.'

Bernie and Christine Cropley filleting fish at the rear of Jones' Fish Shop in St. Peter's Street which they ran from 1976 until 1992. The shop was previously owned by the Jones family whose name it still retains today although the present owners are Mr and Mrs Davis. 'Snelly' Rose, who was a relative of mine, had the shop before the Jones' and apparently there has been a fish shop on that site since 1883 although the fish house at the rear is older still and used to stand alone in a field called Jacob's Meadow, in the days when the present shop was a wine house.

Ernie Thompson pictured in 1985 on the Trawl Dock. Ernie, who sadly died recently, began his career at sea as a drifterman in the 1930s and went on to become the only skipper to win the Prunier Trophy twice, the trophy being given to the vessel who brought the largest quantity of herring caught in a single night to the port of Yarmouth or Lowestoft.

He first won the trophy in 1952 at the age of thirty-two, when he skippered the drifter *Lord Hood*, with what was then the biggest herring catch on record, a massive 314¾ crans (about 1000 fish to the cran) which had taken fifteen hours to haul. He repeated his success again in 1958, albeit with a somewhat smaller haul of 162 cran, whilst in command of the drifter *St. Luke*.

For many years he was also a successful trawler skipper, commanding the *Boston Hornet* and he skippered the experimental purse seiner *Princess Anne* and later took over the *Boston Viking*. Ernie Thompson never lost his love of the sea, and he even had glass panels in the front door of his Pakefield home depicting some of the many vessels on which he had worked in a long and varied career.

For many years before the war a familiar landmark in the harbour was a huge tripod known as the 'sheerlegs'. Erected in the 1850s this was a lifting apparatus originally used for hauling out boilers for cleaning from cattle vessels trading between Lowestoft and Denmark and later for those of steam drifters. They were also used for stepping and unstepping masts.

However by 1938 the sheerlegs had outlived their usefulness and on 1st May of that year they were felled by the George Overy company. Preparations were made beforehand by excavating round the foundations and early on that Sunday morning under the direction of Mr A.G. Nightingale, the Harbour Works Superintendent, the structure was tipped and after a given signal it fell into the harbour from where it was retrieved and later cut up for scrap iron.

Two men came within inches of death when a dramatic accident occurred in the yacht basin on Tuesday, 16th September 1980. The pilot boat which had been repaired after sinking at her moorings the previous week was being lowered back into the water by two William Overy cranes, a 12 tonner with Clifford Pitchers in charge and a 15 ton crane operated by Alan Carter.

Mr Leslie Holland, a marine engineer, and Trinity House superintendent Ray Hooker were standing on the deck of the pilot boat when the 15 tonner toppled over causing the jib to smash into the craft which in turn fell onto a small eel fishing boat. Fortunately there was no-one aboard at the time.

Mr Holland said, ". . . Suddenly there was a jolt . . . then she dropped down with a rush . . . As the boat dropped the jib crashed across it. Just a moment before Mr Hooker and I had been standing there but we had just moved away. If that jib had hit us we would both have been mincemeat." As it was the two men were able to scramble clear and were taken to Lowestoft Hospital for a check-up.

Mr Frederick Carr, who was sitting in his boat only feet from where the crane crashed down, said, "How those two men escaped I don't know. They said I would be all right where I was. And I was – but only just!"

The Lowestoft lifeboat, *Frederick Edward Crick*, moored in the yacht basin, with the buildings in Waveney Drive in the background showing the premises of Boston Deep Sea Fisheries with its distinctive mural on the far right.

The *Frederick Edward Crick* was stationed at Lowestoft from 1963 to 1986 and was launched 239 times saving 103 lives. After being withdrawn for repairwork in 1982 and another lengthy refit in 1984-5 it was announced that she was to be withdrawn, her last launch taking place on January 29th 1986 and shortly afterwards was sold out of service. She was replaced by *The Spirit of Lowestoft*, the money for the new boat being raised by the people of the town.

14

This heavy road transporter took nearly fifteen minutes to inch its way from the South Quay to the main road as it began its journey to Sizewell nuclear power station on Monday, 17th June 1963. At 115 feet in length and with a width of 13 feet the massive load needed a police escort. It is pictured here passing the *Royal Hotel* in Marine Parade.

Aerial view circa 1930, showing the *Royal Hotel* (centre) and its three acres of private grounds with gardens, tennis courts and putting green. Directly behind the hotel is the Palace cinema, opened in 1914, and to its right the Yacht Club, leading to the South Pier.

Built by Sir Samuel Morton Peto in 1849, the *Royal* was one of the best hotels on the east coast. Royalty and nobility dined there and in 1857 the *Royal Hotel* was considered to be, ". . . situated at the northern end of the noblest of Esplanades in the United Kingdom, a handsome building offering first class accommodation to travellers of the highest rank . . ." In 1931 a single room cost 7/6d, a double 15/-. Breakfast was 3/6d, luncheon 4/-, tea 2/6d and dinner 6/-. Boarding terms were from one pound a day.

The seaward face of the *Royal Hotel*. Despite extensive refurbishments in 1954, such as removal of the verandahs and the extension of the dining room and cocktail bar, over the next two decades the hotel suffered something of a decline and the final blow came in the early 1970s when the building failed to conform to fire regulations. The estimated £40,000 to put it right was not forthcoming and it seemed cheaper to pull the building down. Many suggestions were made for the use of the building which had a wonderful sea front site, such as a Christian college, a conference centre, a bowling alley, an amusement arcade, a casino and a police station. However, these plans came to nothing and in 1973 the *Royal Hotel* was demolished and its site remained clear until 1993 when the East Point Pavilion was built there.

A photograph of the South Pier and the surrounding area taken during the 1950s. The pavilion, or Reading Room as it was known, was built in 1888, its predecessor having been destroyed by fire three years earlier. The pier with its pavilion had long been a recognisable feature of Lowestoft, and as late as 1938 an average of 10,000 people would promenade along its length every Sunday in summer. However, by the time this photograph was taken, the old structure had fallen into a state of disrepair and was demolished in 1954.

A view of the south beach in the early 1900s, looking north, showing Lowestoft in its Edwardian heyday, with a busy beach, bathing machines, the Esplanade, and the South Pier and pavilion on the horizon along with the many masts and sails of the smacks in the harbour.

There were many interesting bye-laws relating to the beach around this time, such as bathing machines having to contain at least six yards of strong rope, maybe to rope the bather to the machine. It seems it was forbidden to give public lectures on the beach and perambulators were not allowed to be wheeled over the flower beds in public pleasure grounds. It was also not permitted to beat rugs or scatter cinders on the beach or to throw stones or sand and there was also an unusual offence termed, 'Wilfully Jostled' which it seems was left open to interpretation!

2369. 10. South View, and Wellington Road, Lowestoft.

Wellington Road looking towards London Road South, circa 1905. On the right, between the premises of the photographer Augustus Young and the *South View Hotel*, was an alley leading to the South Lowestoft Swimming Baths, situated in a building which would be converted into the Grand Cinema after the First World War.

In front of the shop belonging to Fisher's Main Dressing Rooms (advertised on the roof of the property) can been seen a tram making its way down London Road South whilst in the foreground is one of the many French onion-sellers who used to be about the town.

Interior view of the South Lowestoft Swimming Bath in London Road South. Originally known as the Victoria Hot and Cold Sea Water Baths and Gymnasium, it was opened on Tuesday, 22nd July 1896 by the Mayor and Mayoress, Colonel and Mrs A.G. Lucas. After the opening ceremony, which took place at three o'clock, there were apparently, ". . . some grand aquatic performances by lady and gentlemen swimmers . . ."

The pool at 90 feet in length was one of the largest in the country with fresh sea water pumped at every tide, heated to a suitable temperature by steam pipes and always clear owing to a double floor. It was equipped with a chute, trapeze, rings and a diving pulpit and an instructor was in daily attendance. There were also private sea water baths.

These premises would later become the Grand Cinema, which opened in 1920 with the emptied pool still under the floor. Currently the building is empty and in a state of ruin after renovations plan were halted.

Two views of St. John's Church in the early 1900s. The top picture taken from the south shows the former vicarage on the left.

St. John's Church

Despite the church being situated in London Road South, the majority of St. John's parishioners came from north of the bridge, with the parish extending from Mill Road to the Marina and west to Rotterdam Road.

The origins of the church lay in Sir Samuel Morton Peto's development of the area to the south of the bridge causing the population of this locality to grow which soon brought about the need for a place of worship for these people. Church of England services had been held in a small building at the bottom of St. John's Road but in 1853 the foundation stone of the church of St. John the Evangelist was laid by John Henry Gurney, M.P. for King's Lynn, and within a year the building was completed.

St. John's was consecrated by the Bishop of Winchester, deputising for the Bishop of Norwich on the 15th July, 1854, having been erected by the nationally famous firm of Lucas Brothers, who had their headquarters on the shore of Lake Lothing. The church was designed by John Louth Clemence and built of Kentish rag stone with Caen stone dressings and had thirty windows, each having a different design. A west aisle was added in 1881, at a cost of £1000, increasing the sittings by 300, and in 1897 the clock was added, supplied by Bonsall's of Pier Terrace to mark Queen Victoria's Diamond Jubilee. In 1904 the church's golden jubilee was celebrated by the replacement of the original Norman & Beard organ with a new instrument which remained in service until the closure of the church. This was where Benjamin Britten was given organ lessons by Mr C.J.R. Colman.

Because of its proximity to the sea St. John's had to be restored in 1928. Four years later the top of the spire had to be rebuilt and in the great flood of 1953 the building suffered severe damage. By the 1960s the soft stone was crumbling badly and by the time of its demolition in 1978 the church had become a ruin.

*Suffolk Hotel
Advert 1905*

Suffolk Corner, looking towards London Road North in the late 1950s. This exposed area was said to be the coldest place in England. The two main features of this view, the *Suffolk Hotel* and Tuttle's have both long since departed the scene. Work began on the demolition of the *Suffolk Hotel* in December 1971 and the site was redeveloped over the next three years before becoming a Lipton's supermarket for nearly a decade. In 1983 Lipton's closed and the premises were acquired by a fast food restaurant.

Tuttle's meanwhile closed in 1981 but the Tuttle family had long since relinquished control of the famous shop - in 1960 it had been sold to Debenham's although the name remained. The building has now been converted into smaller units as it was before Tuttle's grew and acquired the little shops around them after their arrival in 1888.

Another change to this view is, of course, the traffic system. In 1978 this area was renamed Station Square and a new road system introduced which involved pedestrianising and landscaping the area shown to the left of Tuttles and the closure of London Road North to traffic.

The fire at the Tuttle's building in July 1964 was centred in the roof above the furniture department which was separated from the rest of the store by Baird's shoe shop and the offices of the General Accident Company. Although untouched by the fire these premises suffered damage from water which came through the roof and were without electricity until the beginning of the following week.

It took one hour and fifteen minutes to get the blaze under control by which time nearly all the roof in the corner section of the building was destroyed. Salvage work began soon afterwards but the ornamental turret, shown in the picture, was demolished after consultation with the local building officer.

Tuttle's Fire

On Friday, 10th July 1964, just before 10.30 am, staff in Tuttle's furniture department on the ground floor heard a noise above them. "We heard this terrific crash," said Mr D.C. Jackson, Tuttle's furniture buyer, "and looking up the stairs I could see the top floor was full of smoke and flame. I think the crash must have been the ceiling of the top floor falling in . . ."

The store was quickly evacuated with around sixty customers and eighty staff joining the gathering crowd on the surrounding pavements as smoke began to billow from the turret on the corner of Tuttle's roof. Some customers however were caught unawares, such as one woman who had been trying on a new dress when the evacuation order was given. She had to continue scrambling into the dress as she left the building where she patiently waited with price tags and washing instructions blowing in the wind. Some customers however refused to panic and one woman was determined to finish her purchase at the toy counter before she would leave.

Within five minutes of the alarm being raised, the Lowestoft fire brigade were on hand to start tackling the blaze as the slates began to fall from the roof and the turret exposing a mass of flames fanned by the strong westerly wind. When the first jets of water failed to reach the turret it was decided to tackle the fire from closer range and a ladder was placed against the building and fireman George Challis sallied forth with his hose, causing consternation among the crowd who could feel the fire's heat from across the road. Fireman Challis stuck to his task though, confronted by the mass of flames, as other firemen tackled the blaze from the back of the roof and within fifteen minutes it was obvious they were subduing the fire.

Seven brigades and sixty-five firemen, over half of which were volunteers, fought the spectacular blaze and although there were no casualties it was described it as the worst fire in the town for a decade.

Looking down Waveney Drive during Tuttle's fire. This road was quickly closed to traffic, and outside the centre of the town vehicles were diverted through Oulton Broad as flames rampaged through the roof section and slates rattled to the ground.

With the fire in the roof finally under control, the firemen and store staff started to move the less badly damaged furniture out onto the quayside and are shown in the photograph piling up the chairs, bedding, ornaments and glassware behind one of the fire engines.

In 1897 Pryce's opened as the Lowestoft Hardware Company in Suffolk Road with four employees. Ten years later the business moved to premises on the opposite side of the road and by the the 1960s, when this photograph was taken, they had expanded into neighbouring properties and employed a staff of one hundred and thirty. This shop was taken over by Godfrey's in 1993.

In the late 1950s part of the west side of London Road North was redeveloped and four new shops were about to be built here. On the left is the same view in the late 1970s, shortly before the main street was pedestrianised. Vehicle access ended in 1981, although the road was still used by buses until May 1983.

Hepworth's corner, in London Road North, circa 1938. On the right is the road to the Marina Theatre. Gallone's ice-cream parlour, on the left of the photograph, was only open two years before it closed at the beginning of the Second World War when the proprietor was interred by the authorities. Most of the buildings in this row, with the exception of Catling's and the United Methodist Church, were destroyed on 13th January, 1942, during the worst air raid on the town, which killed sixty-nine people and left a hundred and fourteen injured.

122-138 London Road North in the early 1950s, showing (from left to right) Kwick Cleaners, Kay's Kitchen, the Lowestoft Co-operative butchery, Doreen's the florist and Electric House, the home of the Eastern Electricity Board.

This row survived the air raids which claimed many of the shops around it and on the left can be seen the start of a bomb site where 142-148 London Road North had once stood.

The photograph (top left) shows the wreckage of Woolworth's which was bombed just after midnight on 5th May 1941. The site was cleared, as shown bottom left, leaving the Eastern Counties booking office standing in isolation. The row was gradually built up again around this little building but in 1987 it too was taken down to be replaced by new retail premises. The United Methodist Church and Catling's store are shown in the distance. The church was damaged in a later air raid and condemned, being finally demolished in 1956, while Catling's made way for the new Fine Fare supermarket in 1980.

CURL BROTHERS,

SUFFOLK HOUSE, LONDON ROAD.
THE LEADING GENERAL AND FANCY DRAPERS.

A Large and Varied Assortment of
NEW SEASON'S GOODS
always in stock to select from.

NOVELTIES IN ALL DEPARTMENTS.

COSTUMES, JACKETS, CAPES, MILLINERY, BLOUSES, SKIRTS, UNDER-
CLOTHING, GLOVES, HOSIERY, RIBBONS, LACES, TRIMMINGS, APRONS,
FALL NETS, DRESSES SILKS, PRINTS, FLANNELS, FLANNELETTES,
LINENS, CALICOES, CHILDREN'S OUTFITTING.

DRESSMAKING, Perfection of Fit and Style Guaranteed,
LEADING FASHIONS! LATEST STYLES! POPULAR PRICES!

Curl Brothers, London Road, Lowestoft.

Advert, circa 1900. The Curl Brother's were situated in these premises from 1892 to 1904.

Suffolk House

For nearly a century a drapery business could be found at 159 London Road North or 'Suffolk House' as it used to be known (not to be confused with the present Suffolk House, London Road North which is on the site of the *Suffolk Hotel*). The earliest record goes back to 1868 when Harvey and Blown had their business here and were listed as linen drapers and silk mercers at Suffolk House, 15 London Road, as it was then known. By 1872 Blown's name had been dropped with Daniel Whittle Harvey continuing to trade here until 1889. By 1892 the Curl Brothers had acquired the premises, remaining there until 1904 when Arthur Legget had his drapery shop here. Horace Frank Roberson took over the shop in 1906 and the family business remained here until 1965 when his son Frank retired and the shop closed, ending the tradition of drapery businesses in these premises.

In the 1970s 'Suffolk House' was no longer a drapery, with Woodhouse Furnishers establishing their business here. In the late 1980s the property became Poundstretcher, a discount store, who have remained here since.

Looking south towards the junction of St. Peter's Street and the High Street. The building in the centre with the arched doorway is Connaught House which, since it was erected in 1814, has been put to a variety of uses, from a Conservative Club to a welfare clinic!

Connaught House

Connaught House was built in 1814 and by the late 1850s the building was occupied by the National Provincial Bank. At that time the premises were owned by a local builder, Robert Brewster, who died in 1869, bequeathing Connaught House to his wife, Margaret Rouse Brewster and, in the event of her death or remarriage, to Alice, the youngest daughter of William Youngman and her heirs. William Youngman, who was to become the first mayor of the town in 1885-86, ran the Youngman's brewery, established 1856, on the corner of Rant Score and was a notable citizen of the town at that time. Around 1870 Benjamin Preston became a partner in his business and two years later married Alice Youngman at Lowestoft parish church. They had a son, Ernest Fortescue Preston, later that year. Unfortunately Alice died in 1875, so when the widow Margaret Rouse Brewster passed away in 1884, the twelve year old Ernest found himself heir to Connaught House.

Ernest would leave the area and lived in Plymouth and Bournemouth around the turn of the century. During this period he leased Connaught House for £65 per annum to the Church of England Incorporated Society who provided accommodation for waifs and strays. The building needed redeveloping for this purpose and when finished was designed to house twenty children and was dedicated by the Bishop of Thetford at the opening ceremony.

Connaught House was sold by Ernest Preston in 1910 to the Mayor, Aldermen and Burgesses of the Borough of Lowestoft for £1,400 and soon after it became a church home for girls. The 1920s saw the building become the Lowestoft Borough School Clinic and the Mother and Child Welfare Clinic and it was part of the Lowestoft Public Health Department for many years, until a new civic development was built in Clapham Road in the mid-1970s.

In 1972 the County Council sold Connaught House to Durrant's the fruiterers who in turn sold the property eight years later to Star Estates Ltd, who redeveloped the building into eight office units, one of which was their own head office.

I shall always remember Connaught House as the Welfare Clinic though, where as children we were marched to see 'Nitty Nora', the nurse who would look in our ears and at our teeth and also comb through our hair for nits. If you did not itch when you went in, you did when you came out!

An advertisement for Devereux & Sons' Stores, dating from around 1900. Founded in 1847 the premises at 127, 128 & 129 High Street were rebuilt in 1869 and underwent further alterations in the early 1900s. The interior was over one hundred feet square and the company had a staff of around sixty assistants in addition to a fleet of vans to make daily deliveries to the town and outlying areas.

The company's warehouses were in Old Market Plain and at the beginning of the twentieth century had stables in Arnold Street. There was another branch, known as Kirkley Stores, situated at 156 London Road South. Devereux' closed in 1973.

Looking north up the High Street in the early 1950s. Prior to the Second World War the wool-shop had previously been a long established stationers and printers originally owned by Arthur Stebbings in the late 1800s. Stebbings, who was a mayor of the town, also published local books. This property is currently Northend Antiques.

The Halifax Building Society, pictured here on the left at 148 High Street, moved to new premises in London Road North in the mid-1950s. Subsequently this building became the Lowestoft Division Conservative Association's headquarters and more recently was the Carpenter's Shop.

An earlier view of the same area is shown on page 43.

Polish Joe

I receive many enquiries from all over the world for information about Lowestoft. It must be a popular place! In early July 1998 I received a telephone call from Bruce Harkness, Professor of English at Kent State University, Ohio, and President of the Joseph Conrad Society who was visiting the town to try to find any details about Joseph Conrad, the great Polish-born novelist, who first set foot on British soil at the port of Lowestoft on 10th June, 1878.

When 'Polish Joe' disembarked from the British freighter, *Mavis*, he was twenty-one and unable to speak a word of English but the seaman signed on as a crew member of the *Skimmer of the Sea* whose master, Capt. Isaiah Munnings gave him his first English lessons.

"We know more about his time in Borneo than in Lowestoft," Mr Harkness told me when we went for tea at 'The Larder' in the High Street. He did at least find out during this visit that Conrad's home while he was in the town was the *Crown and Anchor Hotel* in the High Street, which was owned from around 1858 by George Ward Stebbings and was subsequently kept in the family until 1969, shortly after which it became an off-licence.

The man who came to mind was Roy Stebbings the butcher whose premises are part of the old *Crown and Anchor* building in the High Street. We had a good yarn with Roy but although he was a relation he couldn't help us with any further information. Prof. Harkness half-joked that he hoped Roy might have George Ward Stebbings diary of 1878, perhaps with the entry, 'met a crazy Polish guy today,' but it wasn't to be!

What we do know is that for ten weeks from 11th July to 2nd September Conrad, or Josef Teodor Konrad Korzeniowski to give him his Polish name, served on the coaster *Skimmer of the Sea*, for wages of a shilling a month, making three round trips between Lowestoft and Newcastle. The small ship was operated by seven men, all English with the exception of Conrad who, aside from the cabin boy, was the youngest on board.

I was also able to tell Professor Harkness something about Isaiah Munnings, Conrad's inspiring teacher, who must have been something of a local character. He had four sons, George, James, John and Isaiah and when they came of age he gave each of them a schooner in which to sail the world. Only John resisted the call of the sea, becoming headmaster at Morton Road School in Lowestoft. George sailed the world in the schooner *Archimedes*, Isaiah junior lost his when it ran aground and James finally gave up when he became King's harbour pilot at Lowestoft. George's son, Richard, was later harbour master at Lowestoft too.

It was for his tuition of 'Polish Joe' that Isaiah Munnings will best be remembered, although who could have guessed just how talented his young pupil was. In his own lifetime Joseph Conrad would be best known as a writer of sea stories but it is his novels such as *Nostromo, Heart of Darkness* and *Lord Jim* which have become classics for which he is now admired.

Despite the shortness of Conrad's stay, it seem that the town won a lasting place in his affections. He was even said to have considered Lowestoft to be the place where the finest English was spoken! Of course, as Professor Harkness found out, there is little evidence to be found of Conrad's association with the town now, although Lowestoft has at least named a road after a man regarded as one of the major novelists of the century.

The *Skimmer of the Sea*, the vessel which Conrad served upon during his time in Lowestoft, fared less well.

With a different master, a Captain Cook who lived in Rembrandt Villa in Stanley Street, the vessel sailed from South Shields with a cargo of coal along with another brig named *Neva*. Neither vessels nor crew were heard of again. Captain Cook, who was sailing with a relative, Captain Henry Carr, left a family of four sons and four daughters. After the disaster a large plaque commemorating the two men was erected in St. Margaret's church and this poem was written as a memorial;

Skimmer of the Sea

(Lost October 13th 1881 in a gale)

Where is the *Skimmer of the Sea?*
We wonder where that ship can be.
We know from Shields she set sail
Before that great October gale
To Lowestoft she was bound;
Her home port she has not found.
Ships that left two days behind
They're into port with favouring wind.
Better ship there could not be
Than was the *Skimmer of the Sea.*
She had a crew and captain brave
That ever sailed the ocean wave.
Widows now in grief do mourn
For those who never can return.
The little children ask and say
'Why do Papa so long delay?'
Your dear papa will come no more
To cheer you as he had before,
Until the day that God has said
The ocean shall yield up its dead.

This view of the High Street shows the place where Joseph Conrad stayed in the 1870s. *The Crown and Anchor* is shown to the left of the photograph, next door to the *Crown Hotel*.

General view of St. Peter's Street, looking east towards the High Street. On the right, behind the branches can be seen Greaves' Bakery, which stood on the corner of Tennyson Road, while Chapel Street is the road leading off to the left. All of these buildings were demolished and the site cleared in the mid-1960s to make way for a new road scheme.

(Right)
Old Market Plain in the 1950s. Towards the end of this decade the buildings were taken down and the site cleared to make way for a block of flats and a car park and, later, a new road.

Although quite a busy centre before the last war, the heyday of the Old Market Plain was in the late nineteenth century when a mixture of trades could be found here including a greengrocer, a toy shop, a bonnet maker, a tailor by the name of Copping and also Cable's barber shop. There were two pubs, the *Old Market Inn* which survived until the demolition and is pictured on the left of the photograph, and the *Black Swan* which was situated in the building towards the centre, behind the old gas lamp. Old Market Street leads off to the right.

(Right, inset)
A 1950s view looking down Old Market Street into the High Street. The *Globe Hotel* can be seen at the far end on the left and the dark building in the background is part of Flint House. Just to the left of the lamp-post in Old Market Street is Edward Ansdell's 'tripe shop' although Mr Ansdell was listed as a 'tripe dresser' in the local directories which is perhaps how he would have preferred his business to be described.

Nellie Giles' shop was situated at 43 Duke's Head Street for many years and is pictured here shortly before its demolition in the early 1960s. This was typical of the kind of shops which were dying off at this time and bore few similarities to retail outlets today. Many were situated in the front rooms of houses and they were mostly little family businesses handed down through the generations.

The corner shops would always have a wonderful selection of sweets and Nellie Giles' shop is shown here advertising 'Fry's Celebrated Chocolate' and 'Rowntree's Chocolates and Pastilles'. In the 1930s shopkeepers would serve loose sweets in paper cones which were made from squares of newspaper ready cut on the counter. Even if you only had a farthing (a farthing being a quarter of an old penny) it was a real treat to buy sweets.

The Gotts family ran the Crown Stores which was situated in Crown Street. These premises, along with the neighbouring Crown Cafe and the *Rose and Crown* public house were demolished in the 1960s.

The demolition of Mariner's Street on December 30th 1958. There were many old houses in this area that were removed as part of the slum clearance programme of this period. Emery's bacon shop can be seen on the far side of the road in the distance and would shortly join the rest of the surrounding properties in a pile of rubble.

Pakefield Cliffs in the late 1930s. By this time, the coastal erosion which had threatened Pakefield all century had started to slow but unfortunately by 1938 the thirty five feet of land which had been lost during this decade was inhabited land, and here we see the last vestiges of the street known as 'The Avenue' disappearing into the sea.

The photograph shows the building of the Jubilee Wall, which began in 1935, costing £54,410. The cliffs continued to crumble into the sea though causing the need for further work to be carried out in 1942, even though there was a war on. Thankfully this seems to have stopped the erosion and the cliffs have remained more or less the same since.

Another view of the cliffs at Pakefield, with a ruined property even closer to the edge. The flag hanging over the cliff was used to warn people on the beach below that another landslide was imminent.

Ned's Yarn

While were on the subject of Pakefield, this tale about the *Turnkey Inn* was told to me by my old mate, Ned. It is recounted that at one time in Pakefield, beyond the area of Beach Street and what was to become the ill-fated Cliff Gardens Estate, was the *Turnkey Inn*. It is believed that the inn had been established there for hundreds of years but the surrounding land had gradually disappeared due to coastal erosion and by the eighteenth century the inn was sitting perilously close to the edge of the cliff. Its landlord,

Mr Obadiah Harrison, refused to leave the building or resite the inn as ". . . there will always be a *Turnkey Inn* . . ." and despite the building's precarious cliff-top position, its popularity was undiminished.

It is said that in the year 1711, on the night of 'a most fearsome storm' the *Turnkey's* regulars resolutely disregarded the elements to spend a night in their favourite drinking house. However, for all who did it was to be their last night for when the villagers of Pakefield gathered the following morning to look for missing fathers, sons and daughters, no trace of the building was found, not even rubble on the beach. No-one even heard or saw the landslide. It seemed the sea had swallowed the *Turnkey Inn* whole!

In the following years the inn became legendary amongst sea-faring folk and many myths arose out of its disappearance. Some time later, around the mid-1700s, a local fishing boat was out at sea in a thick dense fog. Night was descending and the men were tired and about to pull up their nets and head for home. Suddenly one member of the crew noticed a faint noise coming from a northerly direction. Then another member of the crew spotted some lights coming towards them. They screamed to the rest of the crew to come up on deck as the strange apparition moved towards them. For what appeared to be a building, yes a building, was floating through the mists. The skipper shouted, "It's the *Turnkey Inn!*" and the crew watched in amazement as the inn floated past the boat as if it were a vessel too! It is recorded that one crew member said he had caught a glimpse in the window of the inn as it passed him and everyone appeared to be in high spirits, and he vividly remembers the raucous laughing and singing coming from the building. The inn floated by and then returned to the mists as quickly as it had come, leaving the crew of the fishing boat dumbstruck.

One has to remember, when considering the fantastic nature of this tale, the words of the landlord, Mr Obadiah Harrison, who vowed that there would always be a *Turnkey Inn*. Perhaps he was right and the inn does still exist, haunting and sailing the North Sea with a never-ending supply of good liquor and high spirits.

Furniture being removed from the original *Wherry Hotel*, ready for rebuilding work to begin in 1899. An advertisement for the original establishment, which had earlier been known as the Wherry Inn Yachting House, boasted of a bowling green and garden, good stabling and coach horses, sailing and angling boats, fishing tackle, boat mooring and men. There was also a saloon, smoke room and museum.

The hotel has continued to be redeveloped over the years and now adverts for the *Wherry Hotel* talk of conference, banquetting and wedding facilties, with discos, bars and accommodation but still boat mooring!

Skating on the Broads in February 1963. In the early 1960s there seems to have been a period of snowy winters, as the previous year there had been a barbecue and bonfire on the ice, the first time that such an event had been held here since a bullock had been roasted on the frozen Broad in 1891. I can remember the severe winter of 1947, when rationing was still with us. The coal ration was meagre, there were power cuts and food was far from plentiful. One memory was seeing the women and children with old prams queueing outside the old gas works on the Beach Village in the hope of buying a load of coke. It was an unforgettable winter and although there was skating on Oulton Broad that year, we did not get a lot of fun out of that icy snap. There are always those who get carried away by the thickness of the ice on Oulton Broad and there were even occasions when some folk enjoyed the rare experience of driving their cars over the Broads!

Bridge Road, looking from the Congregational Church to St. Mark's Church in the early 1900s. St. Mark's was erected in 1884 at a cost of £1,700 on land given by George Edwards, a local J.P. The church was originally built as a Chapel of Ease to St. Peter's Church in Carlton Colville but in 1931 St. Mark's own parish was constituted.

The Congregational Church was built in 1858 with sittings for one hundred. The 'temporary' extension was erected in 1897 but stood for over ninety years until the church was demolished as part of the Oulton Broad relief road scheme by which time it had been taken over by the Free Presbyterian Church whose new building is in Victoria Road.

Looking towards the North Station at Oulton Broad, circa 1950. The station's footbridge, which can be seen in the distance, was taken down in 1973 because it was proving too costly to maintain. On the right can be seen Durrant's, the newsagent, with Mr Clarence Durrant standing in the doorway with Mr Reed. This business was situated in these premises on the corner of Bridge Road and Harbour Road until the late 1960s, when it was taken over by J. & T. Willis.

(Left)
Victoria Road in the 1920s, seen from Bridge Road. The antiques shop on the left belonged to William 'Clockwork' Brown and was situated at Nos. 13 & 15. Also in this row, were Beckett's confectionery shop at No. 21 and Mobb's the fishmonger, at No. 29. In the late 1930s Peter Baxter, the carpenter, also had his premises here, at No. 27. The corner shop which can be seen on the right belonged to Herbert Beare, who was a butcher and green grocer.

A 1902 picture showing part of the collection of Mr J.H. Yallop, described as 'genuine old Lowestoft soft paste in colour'.

In 1863 a description of Lowestoft porcelain tells us, "The early ware was of a very ordinary description and the ornamentation very rudely painted, and in blue; but in their more recent manufactures they made a fine porcelain which was painted extremely well; the intricacy of the patterns, and the minuteness of execution entitling them to be placed in the cabinets of connoisseurs, amongst either Sevres, Dresden or Worcester."

One of the best painters at the factory was a French refugee by the name of Thomas Rose. He was known for painting red roses and twinned chains of rosy wreaths, and he was said to have lived in one of the two cottages, 25 and 27 Crown Street, which were pulled down on March 28th, 1948.

It is not known what part of France this man came from or even when he died. Rumour had it that at one time he had estates in France worth millions and that he was a descendant from royalty in his own country. However, his eyesight failed and he ended his days as a water-carrier using a couple of old donkeys that that been given to him. My family were adamant that they were descended from Thomas Rose and this does seem likely as it is known he had a son, born in 1778, also called Thomas, who became a fisherman.

Lowestoft China Factory

(Right) The front elevation of the Lowestoft China Factory in Bell Lane, now known as Crown Street and (below) all that was left of the original building, the rear wall in Factory Street, which was later demolished and rebricked for Winsor and Newton's brush factory.

The Lowestoft China Factory opened in 1757 and continued until around the end of that century. The greatest prosperity was between 1770 and 1780, towards the end of which period between 60 and 70 persons were employed.

Towards the end of the nineteenth century some people began to doubt that there had ever been an important porcelain works in Lowestoft. All these arguments were settled in 1902. While an air shaft was being installed in the building then standing on the site of the old factory quantities of moulds and bits of china were found, proving once and for all that work had been carried out in the town. Today Lowestoft porcelain is known and admired all over the world and is highly sought after.

The Lowestoft War Memorial Museum, dedicated to all those who served in or from the Lowestoft area during the Second World War, including civilians and volunteer services. Lowestoft was one of the most badly bombed coastal towns and the museum has a large photographic display showing the destruction caused and also has many items of wartime memorabilia, including model boats and planes, badges and medals, and even shells and hand grenades! The Museum is staffed by an eager team of volunteers, made up of Stan and Hazel James, Keith and Barbara Lewis, Ernie and Joan Betts, Ivan and Joyce Meadows, John Ayers, Janet Sillett and Marian Chipperfield, all of whom I am grateful to.

The Lowestoft War Memorial Museum

It was in the early 1990s that I approached the councillors through Peter Waring, the Amenities Officer, about the possibility of obtaining premises in which to establish a War Memorial Museum and was offered the building previously used by the gardeners in the Sparrow's Nest Park.

I was invited to inspect the building with representatives from Waveney District Council, Stella Bostock, Jack Reynolds, Peter Waring, Shirley Preston and Jenny Raho, and we found it to be very dilapidated and needing thousands of pounds spent on it. Everything one touched or looked at needed repair work. There was one room that had been used as an office by the Suffolk Wildlife Trust that wasn't too bad but the entrance hall and another room were full of lawnmowers, diesel oil, gardeners' tools – forks and shovels all over the place. Upstairs, via a rickety staircase, was where Waveney District Council kept old records and props for the Marina Theatre. The building was in an appalling condition, needing floors, ceilings and roof repairs, and it seemed no maintenance work had been carried out there since the end of the war.

When people heard that I was thinking of taking over the building and had a look round for themselves they said I was mad, daft and crazy, saying it would take over £30,000 to put it in order! In fact, it did cost £23,000 which I somehow had to raise. Waveney District Council was quite happy for me to have the building but over the next two years when I had only managed to raise £2,000 the project seemed to be going nowhere. It was then that I happened to meet a great friend of mine, Keith Bryenton Rochard, who seemed interested in my idea and met me at Sparrow's Nest to view the building. He had a look round and took me aback when he said, "Let's get started!"

I was slightly dubious about starting because of our lack of money and I do not think I would have gone any further but for Keith's confidence that the building could be done up. He insisted that I contact the Council to say that we would like it and in September 1994 we began the slow job of renovating the old place.

At first it was just the two of us and his son Andrew and there were many obstacles facing us. A few weeks later I began to despair again after we were told what we could do and what we couldn't do. Eventually we knuckled down and abided by the laws and regulations and soon more of my old friends turned up to help and we had a working team consisting of Stanley James, Lenny Cook, Douglas Smith, Ronnie Wilson and Ivan Meadows, all of whom were pensioners. There were also young ones who helped, David Emery, Andrew Rochard and his brother James, Keith's sons. James helped to rewire the museum and also fitted fire and burglar alarms. None of these volunteers would accept any money at any time, the reply I always received was that they had done it for me. What friends to have!

As we progressed with the building Boulton and Paul supplied us with all the fire doors and double front doors, and the iron framed windows came from the old Roman Hill School buildings in Avondale Road which were then being demolished. By this time Keith was urging me to plan how I wanted the rooms laid out. After deliberation I decided that the first room downstairs should be the A.R.P. room, containing gas masks, helmets, A.R.P. leaflets, ration books, identity cards, clothing books and many more items with the walls covered with posters and photographs of the bombing of Lowestoft. When this room was completed Keith was then asked to make a small room into a Chapel of Remembrance. This he did and I was completely overcome by the way he transformed the room into the beautiful chapel it is today. Many hundreds of people have attended the museum just to see the chapel and they always remark how beautiful it is. Also on show in the museum is Ernie Childs' wonderful depiction of an air raid.

It was just about this time that Jane Jarvis, a trustee of the Museum, offered her help and quickly became indispensable. I can honestly say that she has been like my right arm! We certainly needed her as the work and fund raising continued.

Next was the renovation of the staircase, transformed by the team of volunteers. At the top of the stairs was a large room which we divided into two rooms; one is now dedicated to the First World War and the other is a Battle of Britain room. All ceilings, windows and doors were renewed by the team of volunteers. These men and boys really worked hard every time they turned up.

The outside of the building also needed a lot of work. Dougie Smith is pictured on the verandah.

Dougie Smith and Lenny Cook were two members of the working team who helped with the renovation of the old building. They are shown here battening the walls and ceiling ready for the fireboards.

The time came when although the museum was not quite finished, with the large long room upstairs still needing work, the rest of the building was ready and we could open to the public. On Sunday, 7th May 1995, a day before the anniversary of V.E. Day, the Lowestoft War Memorial Museum finally opened.

I will be forever grateful to all those who helped me to achieve my dream and who continue to support and help the museum now that it is up and running. Jane Jarvis still plays a major role in the museum and I certainly value her continuing support. Her husband Basil and her son Robert have also had a big involvement with the project and Robert has loaned the museum a large part of his personal collection of war memorabilia and he was made Curator owing to his interest in the war years. The museum even has its own photographer Bert Collyer, who has printed from old negatives many of the photographs which can be seen adorning the walls.

Brian Soloman, another trustee, has also proved invaluable - always available and willing to help in any way he can. Peter Waring and Jenny Raho, both from Waveney District Council, were always there to help us; whether it was advice or help we needed, they were there. I must also thank Keith and Barbara Lewis for all their time and involvement with the museum and the many tradesmen and everybody else, too numerous to mention, who responded to my call for help, and of course all the volunteers without whose labours the museum could not have taken shape, especially Keith Rochard who organised all the building work and did a supreme job.

I want the museum to be a memorial to all those who served the community, in and out of uniform, to all those who served in and from Lowestoft, and also to all those who gave their lives during air raids or in any theatres of war all over the world.

Remembering

When I see those rows of graves
I think of all of those so brave
Who gave their lives for me and you
So we could see the skies so blue.
The years have gone and time rolls by,
I saw those graves, tears came to my eye.
Faces of boyhood friends came to light
Why, oh why, must nations fight?
My eyes once more fill with tears
When I glance back to wartime years.
I think of words I would love to say,
Please God, hear us, when we kneel and pray.
Protect our children and our kin
By making war one great big sin.

Jack Rose

The Museum also has a small Remembrance Chapel, where
visitors are invited to enter names of loved ones in the book
of remembrance and leave, if they wish, a photograph to be
hung in the chapel. The stained glass window was made by
David Bullock and Eric Church.

The Royal Naval Patrol Service at Sparrow's Nest in the Second World War. The men standing on the lawn are receiving orders from the Commodore and officers in the bandstand. The building which now houses the War Memorial Museum can be seen on the very far left of the photograph.

(Left)
Marching from St. Luke's to Sparrow's Nest at the beginning of the Second World War. The Navy boys are marching in fours so it must be early on in the war as later they had to march in threes because the weight distribution was proving too much for the old swing bridge!

People gather near the *Royal Hotel* and the Palace Cinema for a service of thanksgiving to mark the end of the Second World War.

Picture Index

The King touching his cap to me after I gave him advice on the evacuation of Lowestoft.

Unbeknown to a lot of people, during the war years I was very friendly with King George VI, who often phoned me up when he was concerned with anything. One night when I sat listening to 'Lord Haw-Haw' the 'phone rang so I picked it up and a voice said, "Hello, Boy Jack, how are you getting on, it's George here!"
I said, "Hello George, are you alright?"
"No," he said, "I've got a problem."
"What's the problem, old mate?" I asked.
He said, "Lowestoft might be invaded and if it is we have got all the children running wild about the streets and if an invasion do come they're going to be in the way of our troops."
"That's no problem George," I said. "Evacuate!"
"Evacuate?" he said, "What's that?"
I said, "Round them all up, put them on trains and send them all inland out of the way."
"Cor blast," he said, "why didn't I think of that!?"
So I said, "Don't worry George old mate, we can't all have brains, can we?"
He said, "Right, I'll get in touch with old 'Winnie' Churchill and the cabinet, he always listens to your advice."

A few days later on 2nd June 1941 the children were evacuated from Lowestoft to Derbyshire but little did they know they had me to blame. And that's my story of how the evacuation began. Beat that one Ned!